ENVY &
JEALOUSY
Taming the Terrible Twins

JUNE HUNT

Printed by Regent Publishing Services Ltd.
Printed in China
November 2017, 1st printing

CONTENTS

ear Friend,

Most of us know people who continually crave something they *don't have* or constantly fear losing what they *do have*. These people often struggle with *envy* and *jealousy*—two distinctly different emotions yet both can be equally destructive.

If you're thinking: *This isn't my problem*, believe me, I understand! But before you come to this conclusion, let me share an experience from *my* past when envy unexpectedly reared its ugly head!

When I was 24, I was invited to sing for a charity event at a local country club. Another singer—my mother's friend—would also be performing. This attractive dramatic soprano, a popular, well-traveled soloist, had earned the reputation of always being well-received by audiences.

I appeared onstage first, then came Martha. At the conclusion of her powerful performance, she received a well-deserved round of applause. Immediately, I found myself wondering, *Hmm, how long did her applause last?* This initial thought shocked me: *June, what are you doing—trying to measure her applause to yours? Why are you comparing yourself to Martha?* (I had never had these thoughts before.)

Following the speaker's message about the charity, Martha and I each had another opportunity to sing. I prepared myself by praying, *Lord, I pray that my music will draw people into a deeper dependence on You.*

After my final song, I felt pleased with my heart message communicated through the music. Then as I walked back to my seat, I suddenly became acutely aware of the applause . . . no, the *length* of the applause . . . *for me.* Instantly I felt disgusted. *June, don't do this. Stop it! Stop it!* I was stunned and even saddened at my own desire to be as well-received as this gifted, seasoned soloist. I very much wanted to be content just to do my best.

How interesting, at that moment, it didn't matter that I had a university degree in music (as was also true of Martha). It didn't matter that a year before I had sung on NBC's *Today* show, or that I'd done a USO Tour to Vietnam, or had been guest soloist for the Billy Graham crusades. Obviously, accomplishments and acclaim are not protectors guarding us against the potential emotion of envy.

Regardless of our achievements, envy is the breeding ground for discontentment. However, if we want spiritual growth in our lives, the Bible says, *"Godliness with contentment is great gain"* (1 Timothy 6:6).

Because of that single experience, I've been keenly aware of my own potential to be envious. I'm sure envy has crept into my life since then. Yet, to be honest, I am afraid of it and don't want any part of it! Instead, I want to trust God with whatever He has given me to do, and do it to the best of my ability—without comparing myself to someone else. I know my life isn't based on what I do or what I accomplish. And God certainly doesn't determine my value, or yours, by comparing us to someone else.

We all must be on guard against the "evil eye" of envy. But how? Let me share one suggestion.

In 1986, HOPE FOR THE HEART—our biblical counseling radio ministry—began as a 15-minute program airing one theme each day for a week. Years later, we were advised to increase the length of our daily broadcast to 30 minutes. But we didn't know that another 15-minute program was also expanding to one half-hour the same month. Both programs were often paired together to make a 30-minute block.

Then it appeared that our two programs would be "competing" to be placed on hundreds of stations. (Candidly, I don't like competition in the Christian arena and avoid it like the plague!)

That year when I saw this speaker/radio host at the National Religious Broadcasters Convention, I shared with her that I'd put her name on my bathroom mirror: "I'm regularly praying that you will have the blessing and anointing of God on your ministry." And I meant it. And for three years, I genuinely prayed for her.

Realize, the Bible says, *"Above all else, guard your heart"* (Proverbs 4:23) and *"Pray without ceasing"* (1 Thessalonians 5:17 KJV). Therefore, if on occasion you find yourself struggling with envy or jealousy, make the choice to pray regularly for God's perfect will for that other person. "Lord, I sincerely pray that (_Name_) will be in your perfect will." This one act will help guard your heart. I know—it guarded mine.

Yours in the Lord's hope,

June Hunt

P.S. To guard against destructive envy and jealousy, let Philippians 4:6–7 be a protective shield throughout your life: *"Do not be anxious about anything, but in every situation, by prayer and petition, with thanksgiving, present your requests to God. And the peace of God, which transcends all understanding, will guard your hearts and your minds in Christ Jesus."*

ENVY & JEALOUSY
Taming the Terrible Twins

You've seen many a two-year-old. They stand only knee-high to an adult, yet buck authority with the boldness of a bulldog. Their temper tantrums can topple the firm resolve of many a parent who finally gives in by handing over a toy or a treat. "I'll do anything to stop the squabbling and restore some sense of peace."

The one word two-year-olds never want to hear—except from their own lips—is *No!* This stage of child development, characterized by full-blown selfishness, typically occurs after a child's second birthday. Sometimes it's called *the terrible twos*.

Thankfully, this stage doesn't last a lifetime. However, people of all ages can also experience the tyranny of another trying twosome. If not tamed, the *terrible twins* of envy and jealousy can last a lifetime.

These tyrannical twins are known to dominate and demand. They also hate being told *no*. But if not restrained, envy and jealousy can wreak havoc on relationships and ruin lives.

The Bible conveys this straightforward counsel on the emotion of envy:

> **"Let us not become conceited,**
> **provoking and envying each other."**
> **(Galatians 5:26)**

DEFINITIONS

Imagine a picture from the past. Imagine twin boys who tussle—both inside the womb as infants and outside the womb as adults. And all because these brothers fail to say *no* to the formidable twins of envy and jealousy.

Following a turbulent time in their mother's womb, Esau first enters the world with Jacob right on his heels—his hand literally grasping his brother's heel. The twins seem destined for dissension with their marked differences. Firstborn Esau is a brash, rash outdoorsman while second-born Jacob is a quiet, calculating son who enjoys the craft of cooking. Esau, described as *"hairy,"* is his father's favorite. Jacob, described as *"smooth,"* is his mother's unmistakable favorite. (See Genesis 25:26–27:11.)

However, the twins' greatest struggle is not over their immediate differences, but rather the prized birthright blessing. According to ancient Hebrew tradition . . .

▶ *The birthright* is bestowed immediately at birth to the firstborn son so that following the father's death, this son inherits the leadership role over the family, along with compensation of a double portion of the father's estate (Deuteronomy 21:17).

▶ *The blessing* serves as a "last will and testament" bestowed by the father, and is individualized for each son, usually calling on God's power to accomplish His divine purpose (Genesis 49:28).

▶ *The birthright blessing* is exclusively for the firstborn son related to his status as head of the household, calling on the Lord's guidance for his life and future legacy.

And what a legacy! This legacy would be exclusively to and through the one inheriting this honored role! Promises had already been extended two generations prior—promises not from Abraham, but from God.

God's covenant with Abraham contained guaranteed promises that would be passed down from Abraham to his son Isaac, then to future descendants.

From this one obedient man Abraham, God promises national greatness, national blessing, and a national homeland.

> "I will make you into a great nation . . .
> all peoples on earth
> will be blessed through you . . .
> All the land that you see I will give
> to you and your offspring forever."
> (Genesis 12:2–3; 13:15)

Thus, Jacob, the second born grandson of Abraham, feels intense *envy* toward Esau, who assumes the firstborn rights.

When the twin brothers become young men, the day becomes explosive when hunter Esau returns home with only one thing on his mind—his growling stomach. As soon as he gets a whiff of what Jacob is cooking, he impetuously yells, *"Quick, let me have some of that red stew! I'm famished!"* (Genesis 25:30).

Esau's hungry eyes are fixated solely on the present—the steaming pot of stew. Yet, Jacob's envious eyes stay focused squarely on the future—obsessing on the blessings—if only he can get that birthright. Jacob becomes determined to not let a spoonful of red stew reach his brother's lips until Esau bargains away his birthright.

Finally, to satisfy his physical appetite, Esau foolishly yields his birthright—the inherited promises passed down from Abraham to Isaac and earmarked for Esau. The hungry hunter is willing to satisfy his craving *at all costs,* and that cost will be high! Because Esau belittles the value of his birthright, he falls prey to his brother's envious scheme and blurts out . . .

" 'Look, I am about to die,' Esau said.
'What good is the birthright to me?' . . .
So he swore an oath to him,
selling his birthright to Jacob. . . .
He ate and drank, and then got up and
left. So Esau despised his birthright."
(Genesis 25:32–34)

Ultimately, envy ruins relationships. So what exactly is envy?

▶ **Envy** is feeling resentful about the advantages, possessions, or successes of others, with a desire to possess what they have or to deprive others of what they have.[1]

▶ **Envy** is feeling distress over another's possessions, position, popularity, or power. Envy craves: "I want who you are. I want what you do. I want what you have." Left unchecked, envy can escalate to harboring ill will or acting out against the one envied.

▶ **Envy** in the New Testament is one of several Greek words including *phthonos*, which means "feeling upset at the advantage or prosperity of others."[2]

▶ **Envy** is *coveting* what another has. To *covet* in Hebrew is *chamad,* meaning "to long for, lust after."[3]

When God gave Moses the Ten Commandments on Mount Sinai, His heart was to teach all people everywhere how to live a good and blessed life, a life pleasing to God, reflecting His character, and a life free from the bitter consequences of *coveting.* The last of the Ten Commandments says we are not to covet anything that belongs to another.

**"You shall not *covet* your neighbor's house . . . your neighbor's wife . . . or anything that belongs to your neighbor."
(Exodus 20:17)**

Envy—Always Wrong?

QUESTION: "Is envy ever right?"

ANSWER: No. Envy is an expression of pride rather than faith—and, as such, is always wrong. To envy is to covet—which is expressly prohibited by God in His Ten Commandments. Envy is often accompanied by entitlement: "I'm entitled to have what you have." Even Pilate, a Roman ruler of pagan background, realized the Jewish leaders wrongly accused Jesus because of envy. They envied His astonishing power and popularity with the people. That is why Pilate offered the notorious prisoner Barabbas to be crucified in Jesus' place. The Bible reveals . . .

> **"For [Pilate] knew that they had handed Him over because of envy."**
> **(Matthew 27:18 NKJV)**

WHAT IS Jealousy?

The time has finally come. Isaac, the aged father, is now approaching death. Unaware of the bowl-of-stew-bargain, Isaac tells his firstborn to hunt some wild game. After eating the *"tasty food,"* he will bestow upon Esau the long-awaited birthright blessing.

Overhearing their conversation, mother Rebekah concocts the ruse. This just might work for Jacob, because her husband has now become *blind*. No sooner does Esau leave when Rebekah instructs her favored son, *"Bring me two choice young goats,* so I can prepare some tasty food for your father, just the way he likes it. Then take it to your father to eat, so that he may give you his blessing before he dies" (Genesis 27:9–10).

Yet Jacob's mind is reeling. "*But my brother Esau is a hairy man while I have smooth skin. What if my father touches me?*" (Genesis 27:11–12). As the plot thickens, it seems the hairy goats will be used for more than just tasty stew. Rebekah covers Jacob's hands and neck with goat hair, and tells him to put on Esau's clothes. The setting for the ruse is complete, including the outdoors smell wafting through Esau's clothing.

The deceptive display works. Isaac is tricked into giving Jacob the birthright blessing: *"May nations serve you and peoples bow down to you. Be lord over your brothers, and may the sons of your mother bow down to you. May those who curse you be cursed and those who bless you be blessed"* (Genesis 27:29).

Jacob is barely out of sight when Esau discovers the deceptive plot. He becomes consumed with jealousy when conniving Jacob steals his birthright blessing. Esau spews out his frustration and fury . . .

"Isn't he rightly named Jacob [meaning supplanter or deceiver]? This is the second time he has taken advantage of me: He took my birthright, and now he's taken my blessing!" (Genesis 27:36)

► **Jealousy** is being intolerant of rivalry or unfaithfulness with a desire to be vigilant in guarding what one possesses.[4]

► **Jealousy** in relationships is feeling or exhibiting resentful suspicion when one person is attracted to someone else.

► **Jealousy** in the New Testament is the Greek word *zelos*, meaning "zeal or burning with jealousy."[5]

► **Jealousy** can be a selfish, unhealthy possessiveness based on a sense of owning another person or a fierce, healthy protectiveness of one's rights based on a covenant relationship with that person.

The Bible gives this strong warning . . .

"The acts of the flesh are obvious . . . hatred, discord, *jealousy*, fits of rage . . ."
(Galatians 5:19–20)

Jealousy—Always Wrong?

QUESTION: "I've heard that God is jealous. Isn't jealousy always wrong?"

ANSWER: No. God is not jealous *of* us, He is jealous *for* us. It's natural and normal for feelings of jealousy to surface when a sacred covenant relationship is threatened (such as in marriage or our relationship with God). Out of His great love for us, God *jealously* guards His special relationship with each of us. When giving the Ten Commandments to Moses, these words were spoken: "*I, the LORD your God, am a jealous God*" (Exodus 20:5).

Selfish jealousy arises from insecurity or the belief that one person *owns* another person. *Worldly jealousy* is not based on love, but on wrong desires—self-centered desires to control another person. *Godly jealousy* reveals right desires because they contribute to our lives as God intends them to be.

▶ In the Old Testament, God's righteous jealousy is described in numerous passages.

　■ The name *Jealous* is used in reference to God when His people could become unfaithful and thus not experience His blessing.

"Do not worship any other god, for the LORD, whose name is Jealous, is a jealous God" (Exodus 34:14).

▶ In the New Testament, the idea of *"godly jealousy"* is expressed when the apostle Paul speaks of his deep concern for the Corinthians.

"I am jealous for you with a godly jealousy. I promised you to one husband, to Christ, so that I might present you as a pure virgin to him. But I am afraid . . . your minds may somehow be led astray from your sincere and pure devotion to Christ" (2 Corinthians 11:2–3).

[Note: The Hebrew word *qanah* means *to be jealous* or *zealous*. Likewise, the Greek word *zelos* can be translated *zealous* or *jealous*. Thus, some biblical scholars believe the more appropriate English translation renders God as *zealous* rather than *jealous*.[6]]

After realizing the birthright blessing has been bestowed upon Jacob, Esau becomes red hot with anger and jealousy. Now he has a burning desire to keep what he too easily cast aside. However, he forfeited the right of the firstborn.

Bursting out with "*a loud and bitter cry*," he pleads with his father, "'*Do you have only one blessing, my father? Bless me too, my father!' Then Esau wept aloud*" (Genesis 27:34, 38). But the words that fall from his father's lips are far from those his brother Jacob received: "*Your dwelling will be away from the earth's richness, away from the dew of heaven above. You will live by the sword and you will serve your brother. But when you grow restless, you will throw his yoke from off your neck*" (Genesis 27:39–40).

This worthless blessing contrasted to Jacob's rich blessing causes Esau to explode with jealousy—with angry, deadly jealousy.

> **"I will kill my brother Jacob."**
> **(Genesis 27:41)**

How do *envy* and *jealousy*, words so often used interchangeably, actually differ from one another? The differences are subtle, but distinct.

Envy is . . .	Jealousy is . . .
Empty hands *hungry to be filled*	Full hands *fearing to be emptied*
A burning desire to *get*	A burning desire to *keep*
Craving what *another has*	Clinging to what *one has*
Focused on *gaining*	Focused on *losing*
Fueled by a sense of *entitlement*	Fueled by a sense of *retaining control*
Rooted in ambitious *pride*	Rooted in anxious *fear*
Usually involving *two* people (e.g., you envy someone who has what you want)	Usually involving *three* or more people (e.g., you feel jealous over an outside rival)

What is the ultimate solution to struggling with these painful emotions? The answer is learning to be content with what we have in our lives. Contentment is a wonderful state of satisfaction and serenity, comfort and fulfillment, pleasure and a heart at peace. This comes much more easily for those who yield their lives to the Lord. *"If they obey and serve him, they will spend the rest of their days in prosperity and their years in contentment"* (Job 36:11).

Envy means we do not trust God to give us what we need, while *jealousy* means we fear God will take from us what we truly need. Both stand in opposition to God's character. Both are contradictions to who He is—our gracious, generous God; our faithful, forgiving Father; our Lord who not only is *love*, but also who only acts out of His love for us. He cannot act in contradiction to His character. This is why we need to know God's heart on these two painful emotions.

> **"How priceless is your unfailing love,**
> **O God! People take refuge**
> **in the shadow of your wings."**
> **(Psalm 36:7)**

God's Heart on Envy

▶ GOD WARNS US:

- **Envy** comes from the heart and is evil.

  "For it is from within, out of a person's heart, that evil thoughts come—sexual immorality, theft, murder, adultery, greed, malice, deceit, lewdness, envy, slander, arrogance and folly" (Mark 7:21–22).

- **Envy** corrupts a person.

  "All these evils come from inside and defile a person" (Mark 7:23).

- **Envy** resides in sinful flesh.

"The acts of the flesh are obvious: sexual immorality . . . envy; drunkenness, orgies, and the like" (Galatians 5:19, 21).

- **Envy** reveals selfishness, a life out of order, and ungodly actions.

"For where you have envy and selfish ambition, there you find disorder and every evil practice" (James 3:16).

▶ **GOD INSTRUCTS US:**

- **Don't** yearn for anything that belongs to another person.

"You shall not covet . . . anything that belongs to your neighbor" (Exodus 20:17).

- **Don't** desire what the ungodly have, and don't seek their friendship.

"Do not envy the wicked, do not desire their company" (Proverbs 24:1).

- **Don't** allow yourself to crave more and more but rather to give more and more.

"All day long he craves for more, but the righteous give without sparing" (Proverbs 21:26).

- **Don't** obsess over what others have—focus instead on how you can give love to others.

"The commandments, 'You shall not commit adultery . . . murder . . . steal . . . covet,' and whatever other command there may be, are summed up in this one command: 'Love your neighbor as yourself' " (Romans 13:9).

God's Heart on Jealousy

▶ **GOD WARNS US:**

- **Jealousy** can lead us to anger and revenge.

  "Jealousy makes a man furious, and he will not spare when he takes revenge" (Proverbs 6:34 ESV).

- **Jealousy** is a powerful force too strong for us to withstand.

  "Anger is cruel and fury overwhelming, but who can stand before jealousy?" (Proverbs 27:4).

- **Jealousy** and quarreling go hand-in-hand when we follow the world's way, not God's way.

  "Since there is jealousy and quarreling among you, are you not worldly? Are you not acting like mere humans?" (1 Corinthians 3:3).

- **Jealousy** in God is aroused when we let someone or something take the place that He alone should have.

  "They angered him with their high places; they aroused his jealousy with their idols" (Psalm 78:58).

▶ **GOD INSTRUCTS US:**

- **Jealousy** over someone straying from devotion to Christ is godly jealousy.

  "I am jealous for you with a godly jealousy. I promised you to one husband, to Christ, so that I might present you as a pure virgin to him" (2 Corinthians 11:2).

- **Jealousy** ignored in our hearts will be met with stern discipline.

  "I fear that there may be discord, jealousy, fits of rage ... On my return I will not spare those who sinned earlier or any of the others, since you are demanding proof that Christ is speaking through me. He is not weak in dealing with you, but is powerful among you" (2 Corinthians 12:20; 13:2–3).

- **Jealousy** can be diffused by repenting and renouncing sinful attitudes and actions.

  "This is what the Sovereign Lord says: Repent! Turn from your idols and renounce all your detestable practices" (Ezekiel 14:6).

- **Jealousy** can be a fierce protector.

  "Place me like a seal over your heart, like a seal on your arm; for love is as strong as death, its jealousy unyielding as the grave" (Song of Songs 8:6).

Up to this point in the lives of Jacob and Esau, the leading characters are not the twin brothers themselves but the terrible twins—envy and jealousy. Though different and each favored by one parent over the other, these two brothers might have found common ground on which to establish and build a relationship—ground where their differences could be minimized and their similarities emphasized. But that doesn't happen.

Instead, envy and jealousy keep them emotionally disconnected and set the stage for them to inflict harm rather than healing, to destroy rather than defend, to provoke rather than protect.

The end result is complete estrangement with one harboring only hatred and the other fleeing in terror. Whatever positive relationship they might have had is shattered on the jagged rocks of envy and jealousy. It would seem these brothers, who once shared their mother's womb, are destined to live out their lives being dead to one another.

CHARACTERISTICS

Jacob, the deceiver, flees 500 miles to escape being killed by twin brother, Esau. Until that time, nothing even hints that Jacob has any kind of relationship with God. However, on the way he has an encounter with God Himself that transforms his life forever.

God not only pursues him but also blesses him, prophesies over him, and assures him that the promises He gave to Abraham are now given to him.

Never again is there a hint of envy or jealousy on his part, even though he is about to spend 20 years being deceived by his mother's brother, Laban. It seems that his alluring "apples" don't fall far from the same deceptive family tree. Indeed, what goes around comes around. And what we sow, we reap.

> "Do not be deceived.
> God cannot be mocked.
> A man reaps what he sows."
> (Galatians 6:7)

Jacob arrives at his uncle Laban's home and soon falls in love with Laban's daughter Rachel. After working seven years under Laban for the right to marry her, Jacob enters into marriage with his beloved—so he thinks. But no! Laban switches younger daughter Rachel for older daughter

Leah. Ultimately, Jacob the deceiver himself gets deceived.

A week later, Laban allows Jacob to marry Rachel, with just one requirement: he must work for his father-in-law—another seven years!

Thus, this can be no surprise . . .

> **"His [Jacob's] love for Rachel**
> **was greater than his love for Leah."**
> **(Genesis 29:30)**

WHAT Characterizes Envy?

Imagine the angst. Imagine the envy.

Although Leah is loved less, she bears Jacob's children. Whereas Rachel, who is loved more, is barren with no children. What a perfect breeding ground for those terrible twins—envy and jealousy. The sisters are wives of the same man, with Rachel not only being the love of Jacob's life but also his prize as a labor of love. Jacob works fourteen years to earn her hand in marriage.

Contentment eludes childless Rachel, and envy overtakes her. Motivated by both envy and jealousy, a childbearing contest of sorts ensues. Rachel devises a plan for Jacob to marry her maidservant, who will bear children for Rachel. Jacob complies. Then when Leah sees that she has stopped having children, she does the same and gives her servant to Jacob as a wife (see Genesis 30).

Childless Rachel and loveless Leah continually struggle with comparisons. However, the Bible gives this word of caution about comparison.

> **"We do not dare to classify or compare ourselves with some who commend themselves. When they measure themselves by themselves and compare themselves with themselves, they are not wise."**
> **(2 Corinthians 10:12)**

The Envy Checklist

Answer *yes* or *no* by each question. Then have someone close to you—truthful with you—take the questionnaire *about you*. If any answers differ, discuss your responses. Ask the Lord what truth exists in what the other person says about you.

_____ Do you resent a relationship that someone else enjoys?

_____ Do you feel unhappy over someone's happiness?

_____ Do you secretly resent another's abilities?

_____ Do you feel provoked over another's elevated position?

_____ Do you have hidden feelings of inferiority?

_____ Do you feel perturbed over another person's possessions?

_____ Do you become angered over someone's
success?

_____ Do you belittle the accomplishments or
talents of someone?

_____ Do you make negative comments about
another person's attractive appearance?

_____ Do you pout about another person's
popularity?

_____ Do you secretly rejoice when someone
suffers a setback?

_____ Do you begrudge the blessings that another
receives?

It's easy to be envious of people who seem to have
it all. When someone appears blessed, we too
would like to be blessed. But if we continue to
compare ourselves with others, we can fall into
the trap of envying not only the good, but also
the not-so-good. Keeping our eyes on the Lord as
our Provider—not on what others have—produces
contentment, the antidote to envy and jealousy.

"The fear [reverence] of the LORD
leads to life; then one rests content,
untouched by trouble."
(Proverbs 19:23)

Two sisters who *could* be close, choose to embrace envy and jealousy rather than each other. Instead of sharing one another's joys and sorrows—instead of seeking an endeared relationship—they engage in resentment and rivalry.

If you have a relationship that is being torn apart by jealousy, honestly evaluate your thoughts, motives, and actions before the Lord. Heed the following words found in the book of Job . . .

> "Teach me what I cannot see;
> if I have done wrong,
> I will not do so again."
> (Job 34:32)

The Jealousy Checklist

Answer *yes* or *no* on the following checklist. Then ask someone who knows you well—someone trustworthy and truthful—to take the questionnaire about you. If any of your answers differ, discuss the reasons for your responses. Ask the Lord to reveal any hidden truth to you.

_____ Do you feel overly possessive of someone or something?

_____ Do you attempt to control others?

_____ Do you want an exclusive relationship with someone?

_____ Do you expect another person to limit outside relationships because that is your desire?

_____ Do you feel anxious over any potential loss of someone or something?

_____ Do you feel threatened that a close relationship might end or change?

_____ Do you assume your worth is tied to someone or something?

_____ Do you feel emotionally dependent on someone?

_____ Do you feel suspicious about the normal behavior of another person?

_____ Do you feel distrustful of others concerning someone (or something)?

_____ Do you feel unable to trust God with the future regarding someone (or something)?

_____ Do you feel insecure when it comes to your future without your possessions, position, power, or other people?

The biblical book on wisdom describes jealous people as those who are out of control and are severely damaging to others. God is saying beware:

"Anger is cruel and fury overwhelming, but who can stand before jealousy?" (Proverbs 27:4)

WHAT Traits Lead to Envy and Jealousy?

Many glance at the words *envy* or *jealousy* and think, *Not me!* But is that true? Doesn't a bit of envy or jealousy periodically appear in all of us? We don't think we have a problem until we catch ourselves *enviously* comparing, competing, or coveting what someone else has or *jealously* clutching, clinging to, or crying over something we fear losing.

The *terrible twins* of envy and jealousy can seem small at first, but when your relationship sours or your contentment disappears or your peace evaporates, you will be wise to take a second look.

Certain traits reveal that envy and jealousy *are* part of our lives. To eliminate these traits, we must examine our lives, acknowledge their presence in our lives, then guard our hearts against them by trusting God with our relationships and generously loving others.

"Let us examine our ways and test them, and let us return to the LORD." (Lamentations 3:40)

Ten Traits That Lead to Envy and Jealousy

▶ **COMPARISON**—Measuring your own worth against someone else's attributes

You say: "If I had his looks, my life would be better. Some people have all the luck."

God says: *"Before I formed you in the womb I knew you, before you were born I set you apart"* (Jeremiah 1:5).

▶ **COMPETITION**—Seeking to outdo or outperform another

You say: "Taking second place isn't an option. I'm in this to win."

God says: *"Don't look out only for your own interests, but take an interest in others, too"* (Philippians 2:4 NLT).

▶ **COVETOUSNESS**—Craving what someone else has

You say: "It's not fair—your parents paid your way. I have to pay my own."

God says: *"Godliness with contentment is great gain"* (1 Timothy 6:6).

▶ **DISCONTENT**—Feeling dissatisfied with what you have

You say: "My car isn't what I want. It can't compare to my friend's car."

God says: *"Be content with what you have"* (Hebrews 13:5).

▶ **FEARFULNESS**—Worrying over a potential loss

You say: "If someone gets laid off, I'm afraid it will be me. Then I will be left in a lurch."

God says: *"Be strong and courageous. Do not fear or be in dread of them, for it is the LORD your God who goes with you. He will not leave you or forsake you"* (Deuteronomy 31:6 ESV).

▶ **INSECURITY**—Fearing an unwanted change or loss in status or circumstances

You say: "After my husband started exercising, I saw other women looking at him. I don't want him around other women."

God says: *"Love is not jealous or boastful or proud"* (1 Corinthians 13:4 NLT).

▶ **POSSESSIVENESS**—Claiming ownership of someone or something

You say: "I'm dating a woman who doesn't always answer my calls. She should always respond as soon as I call."

God says: *"The greedy stir up conflict, but those who trust in the LORD will prosper"* (Proverbs 28:25).

▶ **RIVALRY**—Competing to surpass another

You say: "My brother is a star athlete, but I'll go farther in life because I'm smarter."

God says: *"Those who trust in themselves are fools, but those who walk in wisdom are kept safe"* (Proverbs 28:26).

▶ **SELFISH AMBITION**—Striving to attain a better position

You say: "I don't care who I have to step on to get to the top. I deserve the best."

God says: *"Don't be selfish; don't try to impress others. Be humble, thinking of others as better than yourselves"* (Philippians 2:3 NLT).

▶ **STRIFE**—Engaging in bitter conflict with another

You say: "It's not fair! I'm better, yet *he* gets promoted. He's an idiot! I'm filing a complaint!"

God says: *"They are conceited and understand nothing. They have an unhealthy interest in controversies and quarrels about words that result in envy, strife, malicious talk, evil suspicions"* (1 Timothy 6:4).

Rachel masks her envy and jealousy in self-pity, crying out to Jacob, *"Give me children, or I'll die!"* (Genesis 30:1).

Rachel's sister, Leah, has borne Jacob four sons, a sign of blessing Rachel finds unbearable. Jacob responds angrily to Rachel's ultimatum, *"Am I in the place of God, who has kept you from having children?"* (Genesis 30:2).

Ultimately, Leah and her maidservant provide Jacob with eight sons, Rachel's maidservant provides him with two. And finally, God opens Rachel's womb, and she gives birth to Joseph, his father's favorite son, followed by young Benjamin.

However, the terrible twins—envy and jealousy— take up residence in the lives of Joseph's older brothers who devise an evil plan to kill Joseph. But another opportunity arises, and they sell Joseph into slavery. However, this small band of envious and jealous men cannot circumvent God's call on Joseph's life.

Masking Envy & Jealousy

Those who seethe with envy and jealousy do not like being seen as people controlled by their emotions. Instead, they disguise their negative feelings by putting up false fronts and hiding behind masks to camouflage the truth.

The Bible says, *"You know we never used flattery, nor did we put on a mask to cover up greed—God is our witness"* (1 Thessalonians 2:5).

Common methods people use to hide their envy and jealousy:

▶ **Avoiding** people who could provoke envy and jealousy

▶ **Bringing** up unnecessary, negative information about another person

▶ **Developing** a superior attitude toward someone

▶ **Exaggerating** personal accomplishments

▶ **Fabricating** lies to impress others

▶ **Feeling** self-pity

▶ **Finding** fault in everything someone does

▶ **Idolizing** certain people by placing them on an unattainable pedestal

▶ **Justifying** personal failures

▶ **Majoring** on the unfairness of life

▶ **Offering** false praise and congratulations

▶ **Pretending** to be apathetic or indifferent toward people or situations

▶ **Projecting** jealousy or envy onto others

▶ **Sabotaging** someone else's efforts or plans

▶ **Taking** on the role of a martyr

Conclusion

Ultimately, the rivalry between Rachel and Leah produces twelve sons. The Lord God changes Jacob's name to Israel, and his twelve sons form the twelve tribes of Israel.

While the terrible twins gain access and control over his brothers' hearts, Joseph keeps his mind and heart pure before God and patiently waits for God to work out the plan He has for his life.

Even though he is yanked mercilessly out of his father's life and wrongly sold into slavery; even though he is falsely accused of attempted rape and imprisoned in a dungeon; even though he is forgotten by Pharaoh's cupbearer who promises to remember him to Pharaoh; still Joseph does not surrender to envy or jealousy. Instead, he holds on to his integrity by faithfully serving those in authority over him and trusting God's love and plan for him.

Despite the diabolical schemes envy and jealousy can summon in a person's mind and heart, God can turn even the worst of those into a means of accomplishing the good He intends to bring about in the lives of those He loves.

Thirteen years after Joseph is sold into slavery, he interprets a dream for Pharaoh and is subsequently rescued from prison and placed second to Pharaoh in authority over all Egypt. But it is still another nine years before Joseph lays eyes on his younger brother, Benjamin, and his now much older father, Israel.

All the brothers eventually reconcile with Joseph and he assures them . . .

> **"You intended to harm me,**
> **but God intended it for good**
> **to accomplish what is now being done,**
> **the saving of many lives."**
> **(Genesis 50:20)**

One lesson we can learn from this family's story of envy and jealousy is clear and critical: Keep your eyes steadily and singularly focused on the good God intends and overlook the harm others intend. Only then will you be able to bypass envy and jealousy.

CAUSES

Victory is sweet, but in the presence of envy and jealousy, it doesn't take long for things to go sour. The shepherd boy is the only one brave enough and with faith enough to confront Goliath, the towering giant who stands over nine feet tall, as he taunts the Israeli army and their God.

David approaches the shortsighted scornful enemy not with shining armor, shield, and sword, but with a sling and five smooth stones tucked into his shepherd's pouch. Most importantly, he has the name of the Lord God of Israel on his lips. Only one stone is needed. David courageously runs to battle, loads his sling, and takes his aim. The carefully launched stone lodges in the giant's forehead, and he careens face down on the ground nine feet below.

Within seconds, David has his prize in hand—the Philistine giant's head! Still carrying the head of the once-feared enemy, David is presented before King Saul and heralded as a hero in the nation of Israel. The king is pleased *initially*.

Scripture records many more victories God gives David. *"Whatever mission Saul sent him on, David was so successful that Saul gave him a high rank in the army. This pleased all the troops, and Saul's officers as well"* (1 Samuel 18:5).

The very day of David's victory over Goliath, King Saul whisks him away to the royal palace. Anything David undertakes is met with success, so the shepherd boy-turned-soldier quickly becomes beloved in Israel. All is harmonious with the nation's new hero until the refrain of a song catches the king's ear and instantly kindles the king's anger.

"Saul has slain his thousands, and David his tens of thousands" (1 Samuel 18:7). Saul can't believe his ears. Shamed by his own people exalting someone above him, the refrain reverberates in his head and sends his thoughts spinning.

Satan baits his hook with a song, and Saul takes a bite. Now he dangles from the deadly hook of envy and jealousy, ensnared by words from a simple song sung to praise both king and warrior. Just that quickly, the terrible twosome turns gratitude into greed.

Envy and jealousy begin to consume Saul, and soon crazed behavior characterizes the king's life. " 'They have credited David with tens of thousands,' he thought, 'but me with only thousands. What more can he get but the kingdom?' " (1 Samuel 18:8). And with that thought, paranoia prevails. The situational setup for envy and jealousy is *sealed*. The king has become a slave. *"From that time on Saul kept a jealous eye on David"* (1 Samuel 18:9 NLT).

Envy is . . .

▶ Coveting another's affluence (money, power)

▶ Coveting another's achievement (honors, awards, accomplishments)

▶ Coveting another's appearance (looks, clothes)

▶ Coveting another's abilities (talents, special gifts)

▶ Coveting another's advancement (education, promotions)

▶ Coveting another's activities (trips, social invitations)

▶ Solomon observes, *"I saw that all toil and all achievement spring from one person's envy of another"* (Ecclesiastes 4:4).

Jealousy is . . .

▶ Fearing the loss of attention due to rivalry

▶ Fearing the loss of a relationship due to competition

▶ Fearing the loss of a marriage partner due to marital infidelity

▶ Fearing the loss of parental affection due to favoritism

▶ Fearing the loss of job approval due to competitive work environment

▶ Fearing the loss of social approval due to perceived standards or expectations.

▶ God assures, *"Do not fear, for I am with you; do not be dismayed, for I am your God. I will strengthen you and help you; I will uphold you with my righteous right hand"* (Isaiah 41:10).

WHAT ARE Childhood Setups for Envy and Jealousy?

King Saul detests being compared to David. He cannot stand sharing the spotlight. When Saul's jealousy peaks, he devises a shocking solution.

While David plays the harp, King Saul hurls a spear toward him, plotting, *"I'll pin David to the wall"* (1 Samuel 18:11). Not once—but twice—David dodges danger.

Leading military campaigns, David remains out of Saul's sight, mounting victory after victory. *"In everything he did he had great success, because the LORD was with him. When Saul saw how successful he was, he was afraid of him"* (1 Samuel 18:14–15).

But King Saul is fearful for another reason. He knows the Lord has left him!

Scripture addresses covetousness leading to destructive envy and jealousy.

"You desire but do not have, so you kill. You covet but you cannot get what you want, so you quarrel and fight."
(James 4:2)

Childhood Setups for Envy & Jealousy

Children are likely to develop envy and jealousy if they are raised in homes where they are exposed to some of the following behaviors, which are not only harmful, but can also be abusive.

▶ **Comparison**—comparing one child with another child

"Why can't you be more like your brother?"

▶ **Favoritism**—granting one child favors that are denied another child

"You can stay up late but don't tell your brother or sister."

▶ **Inequality**—expecting more from a son than from a daughter

"Son, your sister is going to walk the dog. I want you to wash the van after you mow the yard."

▶ **Criticism**—finding fault even when a task is performed well

"You made it to the final round of the spelling bee. You could have won first place if you had studied harder."

▶ **Injustice**—punishing one child more than another for the same misdeed

"John, you are grounded for a week, and Joe, don't expect to go anywhere this weekend."

▶ **Performance-based acceptance**—giving acceptance only when expectations are met

"If you forget your lines tonight, I won't take you out for ice cream after the play."

▶ **Conditional love**—giving love only under certain conditions

"If you want me to love you, you better get in there and do your chores."

▶ **Prejudice**—making degrading, disrespectful statements about an individual or group of people

"Those kids are just rich, spoiled brats who don't really care about you. They let you hang around them for their own personal entertainment."

▶ **Discontentment**—never at peace or never pleased no matter the circumstances

"I know this house is nicer than our last one, but it still isn't what I want."

▶ **Entitlement**—expecting something for nothing or expecting preferential treatment

"I should have been the one to win the free vacation to Hawaii because I've never been there."

▶ **Resentment**—begrudging someone for what they have or for what they have achieved

"I can't stand her for being promoted rather than me."

► **Bitterness**—deep resentment and unforgiveness

"I'll never forgive you for what you did, and I'll make sure you pay for it the rest of your life."

► **Preferential treatment**—treating one child better than another

"Emma, since it's Saturday, you're free to spend the day with your friends. Carrie, I expect you to help me clean the house before you go anywhere."

► **Pride**—feeling superior to others and having to always be right

"I make the decisions around here because I always know what is best."

► **Divorce**—further breaking up a family through division of loyalty

"Your father left us to start a new family."

► **Financial instability**—having little income and living from paycheck to paycheck

"I know you want a bike like your friends at school have, but we can't afford the things they have."

► **Self-pity**—feeling mistreated and victimized for no reason

"We never get a break like other people do, so we'll never have a better life and our kids will never amount to anything."

▶ **Materialism**—valuing worldly possessions over intangible ones

"The only way to be happy in this life is to make as much money as you can and enjoy all the pleasures this world has to offer."

These patterns persist into adulthood unless addressed.

"At one time we too were foolish, disobedient, deceived and enslaved by all kinds of passions and pleasures.
We lived in malice and envy, being hated and hating one another.
But when the kindness and love of God our Savior appeared, he saved us, not because of righteous things we had done, but because of his mercy."
(Titus 3:3–5)

No longer grounded by the prophet Samuel or guided by the Spirit of God, discontent dominates King Saul's life. David becomes a man on the run—trying to stay one step ahead of the monarch.

Saul's repeated spiritual failings open the door for envy and jealousy to consume the once rational thinking of a once humble king. David's confusion over Saul's bizarre behavior is expressed in a conversation with Jonathan, his best friend, who also happens to be King Saul's son. *"What have I done? What is my crime? How have I wronged your father, that he is trying to kill me?"* (1 Samuel 20:1).

David and Saul later reverse roles as David has two opportunities for revenge, but refrains from causing Saul harm. Although he could have killed the king, David remains respectful toward the Lord's anointed.

The cat and mouse game ultimately ends when King Saul dies in battle. Critically wounded, he falls on his sword rather than be captured. Now the one Saul feared would become king *does become king*, and a lengthy reign awaits.

**"David was thirty years old when he became king, and he reigned forty years."
(2 Samuel 5:4)**

As with Saul, we lay the foundation for discontent to set up envy and jealousy in our lives by failing to live in right relationship to God.

Causes of DISCONTENT

D ESIRING the approval of others, and failing to be satisfied with the approval of God

BIBLICAL REMEDY

"Am I now trying to win the approval of human beings, or of God? Or am I trying to please people? If I were still trying to please people, I would not be a servant of Christ" (Galatians 1:10).

I NSISTING on God doing things *our* way, and us failing to do things *His* way

BIBLICAL REMEDY

"The LORD detests all the proud of heart. Be sure of this: They will not go unpunished" (Proverbs 16:5).

S EEKING personal significance, and failing to be humble before God

BIBLICAL REMEDY

"When pride comes, then comes disgrace, but with humility comes wisdom" (Proverbs 11:2).

COMPARING ourselves with others and failing to seek to be Christlike

Biblical remedy

"When they measure themselves by themselves and compare themselves with themselves, they are not wise" (2 Corinthians 10:12).

OPPOSING the success of others and failing to acknowledge the achievements of others

Biblical remedy

"Do not withhold good from those to whom it is due, when it is in your power to act" (Proverbs 3:27).

NURTURING selfish gain and failing to make righteousness our goal

Biblical remedy

"Seek first his kingdom and his righteousness, and all these things will be given to you as well" (Matthew 6:33).

THINKING too highly of ourselves and failing to accurately judge ourselves and walk in humility

Biblical remedy

"Do not think of yourself more highly than you ought, but rather think of yourself with sober judgment, in accordance with the faith God has distributed to each of you" (Romans 12:3).

Expecting to impress others by praising ourselves and failing to credit God for working through us

Biblical remedy

"Let someone else praise you, and not your own mouth; an outsider, and not your own lips" (Proverbs 27:2).

Needing to hear praise from others and failing to keep our focus on serving others and pleasing God

Biblical remedy

"We were not looking for praise from people, not from you or anyone else" (1 Thessalonians 2:6).

Taking delight in the misfortunes of another and failing to minister to our enemies through prayer

Biblical remedy

"Do not gloat when your enemy falls; when they stumble, do not let your heart rejoice" (Proverbs 24:17).

WHAT IS a Jealousy Assessment for Relationships?

Jealousy triggers our survival system—the lion in each of us that guards its den and attacks any threat, real or perceived. To arouse strong jealousy is to stir up intense feelings of fear and insecurity that produce the powerful internal reactions of fight, flight, or freeze. To intentionally seek to arouse such jealous feelings can be dangerous to everyone involved.

To the contrary, loving someone is to seek to arouse feelings of security and belonging that produce internal responses of joy, peace, and contentment. What emotions are you evoking in the lives of those you love, and why? What safeguards are keeping you faithful and true?

> **"I made a covenant with my eyes not to look lustfully at a young woman."**
> **(Job 31:1)**

Jealousy Assessment for Relationships

Answer these questions with *yes* or *no* to determine whether or not you need to change, and how much.[9]

_____ Do you intentionally do or say things to cause a jealous reaction?

_____ Does your ego get a boost when your spouse is jealous?

_____ Do you find it flattering when your mate is jealous?

_____ Do you consciously flirt with others?

_____ Do you look at pornography or enjoy entertainment containing sexual content?

_____ Do you often stare at others with lust?

_____ Do you deny staring at others when your spouse catches you?

_____ Do you share complimentary comments with your spouse about members of the opposite sex?

_____ Do your compliments center around physical attractiveness?

_____ Do you have an improper emotional attachment to someone else?

If you answered *yes* to any of the above questions, be honest and confess them to your spouse. Don't say, "You have a problem" or "It's all in your head." Instead, come clean, tell the truth, ask for forgiveness, and work on making the changes necessary to honor your marriage. Write down ways you've contributed to your spouse's insecurity, and then write out a detailed plan to regain trust.

> **"Those who plan what is good
> find love and faithfulness."
> (Proverbs 14:22)**

Jealous Wife

QUESTION: "My wife gets jealous when I harmlessly flirt with other women. How can I make her stop being jealous and accept me as I am?"

ANSWER: Flirting is not harmless. If your wife's jealousy is rooted in your inappropriate behavior, then it's likely not your wife who is doing something she needs to stop, but *you!*

As a husband, it's your responsibility to make sure you give your wife no reason to feel jealous—no reason to feel anything but secure in your love and faithfulness. Don't give her any reason to doubt your commitment to keep yourself for her alone and that includes your eyes and your mind, as well as the rest of your body.

"The heart is deceitful
above all things and beyond cure.
Who can understand it?
'I the LORD search the heart and examine
the mind, to reward each person
according to their conduct,
according to what their deeds deserve.'"
(Jeremiah 17:9–10)

When we go astray in our thoughts and beliefs, we sin and open ourselves up to its consequences. Sinful actions spring from sinful beliefs that are cultivated by sinful thoughts.

> **"The wisdom of the prudent is to give thought to their ways, but the folly of fools is deception." (Proverbs 14:8)**

Three God-Given Inner Needs

In reality, we have all been created with three God-given inner needs: the needs for love, significance, and security.[10]

▶ **LOVE**—to know that someone is unconditionally committed to our best interest

"My command is this: Love each other as I have loved you" (John 15:12).

▶ **SIGNIFICANCE**—to know that our lives have meaning and purpose

"I cry out to God Most High, to God who fulfills his purpose for me" (Psalm 57:2 ESV).

▶ **SECURITY**—to feel accepted and a sense of belonging

"Whoever fears the Lord has a secure fortress, and for their children it will be a refuge" (Proverbs 14:26).

The Ultimate Need-Meeter

Why did God give us these deep inner needs, knowing that people fail people and self-effort fails us as well?

God gave us these inner needs so that we would come to know Him as our Need-Meeter. Our needs are designed by God to draw us into a deeper dependence on Christ. God did not create any person or position or any amount of power or possessions to meet the deepest needs in our lives. If a person or thing *could* meet all our needs, we wouldn't need God! The Lord will use circumstances and bring positive people into our lives as an extension of His care and compassion, but ultimately only God can satisfy all the needs of our hearts.

The Bible says . . .

> "The LORD will guide you always;
> he will satisfy your needs
> in a sun-scorched land
> and will strengthen your frame.
> You will be like a well-watered garden,
> like a spring whose waters never fail."
> (Isaiah 58:11)

The apostle Paul revealed this truth by first asking, *"What a wretched man I am! Who will rescue me from this body that is subject to death?"* and then by answering his own question in saying it is *"Jesus Christ our Lord!"* (Romans 7:24–25).

All along, the Lord planned to meet our deepest needs for . . .

▶ **Love**— *"I [the Lord] have loved you with an everlasting love; I have drawn you with unfailing kindness"* (Jeremiah 31:3).

▶ **Significance**— *"For I know the plans I have for you,' declares the Lord, 'plans to prosper you and not to harm you, plans to give you hope and a future"* (Jeremiah 29:11).

▶ **Security**— *"The Lord himself goes before you and will be with you; he will never leave you nor forsake you. Do not be afraid; do not be discouraged"* (Deuteronomy 31:8).

The truth is that our God-given needs for love, significance, and security can be legitimately met in Christ Jesus!

Philippians 4:19 makes it plain . . .

> **"My God will meet all your needs according to the riches of his glory in Christ Jesus."**

▶ **Wrong Belief**

For Envy: "I have a right to have what others have in order to fulfill my needs to feel loved, significant, and secure."

For Jealousy: "I have a right to keep what I have, what belongs to me, in order to fulfill my needs for love, significance, and security."

▶Right Belief

"I will put my total trust in the Lord and choose to be content regardless of what I have or don't have. He will fulfill my needs for love, significance, and security through His life lived within me."[11]

**"I know what it is to be in need,
and I know what it is to have plenty.
I have learned the secret of being
content in any and every situation,
whether well fed or hungry,
whether living in plenty or in want.
I can do all this through him
who gives me strength."
(Philippians 4:12–13)**

Envy and jealousy can be all-consuming and can lead to catastrophic consequences.

These *terrible twins* will take control if we let them, but the Bible instructs us to allow the Holy Spirit to take control, which leads to the peaceable fruit of righteousness. Only in contentment can we find freedom from destructive envy and jealousy. Only in Christ can we find true contentment.

> "The fear of the LORD leads to life;
> then one rests content,
> untouched by trouble."
> (Proverbs 19:23)

Four Points of God's Plan

Do you want to break free from the terrible twins of envy and jealousy? Do you want God to help you live a life pleasing to Him? And most importantly, do you want to be assured that you will go to heaven when you die? The decision is yours. Will you believe?

> "Yet to all who did receive him,
> to those who believed in his name,
> he gave the right to become
> children of God."
> (John 1:12)

1. **God's Purpose for You is *Salvation*.**

What was God's motivation in sending Jesus Christ to earth?

To express His love for you by saving you!

The Bible says, *"God so loved the world that he gave his one and only Son, that whoever believes in him shall not perish but have eternal life. For God did not send his Son into the world to condemn the world, but to save the world through him"* (John 3:16–17).

What was Jesus' purpose in coming to earth?

To forgive your sins, to empower you to have victory over sin, and to enable you to live a fulfilled life!

Jesus said, *"I have come that they may have life, and that they may have it more abundantly"* (John 10:10 NKJV).

2. **Your Problem is *Sin*.**

What exactly is sin?

Sin is living independently of God's standard—knowing what is right, but choosing what is wrong.

The Bible says, *"If anyone, then, knows the good they ought to do and doesn't do it, it is sin for them"* (James 4:17).

What is the major consequence of sin?

Spiritual death, eternal separation from God.

Scripture states, *"Your iniquities [sins] have separated you from your God"* (Isaiah 59:2).

"The wages of sin is death, but the gift of God is eternal life in Christ Jesus our Lord" (Romans 6:23).

3. God's Provision for You is the *Savior.*

Can anything remove the penalty for sin?

Yes! Jesus died on the cross to personally pay the penalty for your sins.

The Bible says, *"God demonstrates his own love for us in this: While we were still sinners, Christ died for us"* (Romans 5:8).

What is the solution to being separated from God?

Belief in (entrusting your life to) Jesus Christ as the only way to God the Father.

Jesus says, *"I am the way and the truth and the life. No one comes to the Father except through me"* (John 14:6).

"Believe in the Lord Jesus, and you will be saved" (Acts 16:31).

4. Your Part is *Surrender.*

Give Christ control of your life, entrusting yourself to Him.

"Jesus said to his disciples, 'Whoever wants to be my disciple must deny themselves and take up their cross [die to your own self-rule] and follow me. For whoever wants to save their life will lose it, but whoever loses their life for me will find it. What good will it be for someone to gain the whole world, yet forfeit their soul?'" (Matthew 16:24–26).

Place your faith in (rely on) Jesus Christ as your personal Lord and Savior and reject your "good works" as a means of earning God's approval.

"It is by grace you have been saved, through faith—and this is not from yourselves, it is the gift of God—not by works, so that no one can boast" (Ephesians 2:8–9).

The moment you choose to receive Jesus as your Lord and Savior—entrusting your life to Him—He comes to live inside you. Then He gives you His power to live the fulfilled life God has planned for you. If you want to be fully forgiven by God and become the person God created you to be, you can tell Him in a simple, heartfelt prayer like this:

PRAYER OF SALVATION

"God, I want a real relationship with You.
I admit that many times
I've chosen to go my own way
instead of Your way.
Please forgive me for my sins.
Jesus, thank You for dying on the cross
to pay the penalty for my sins.
Come into my life to be my Lord
and my Savior.
Change me from the inside out
and make me the person
You created me to be.
In Your holy name I pray. Amen."

WHAT CAN YOU NOW EXPECT?

If you sincerely prayed this prayer, look at what God says about you!

"His divine power has given us everything we need for a godly life through our knowledge of him who called us by his own glory and goodness."
(2 Peter 1:3)

STEPS TO SOLUTION

The religious leaders *seek honor* with lofty titles and flowing robes, while Jesus *gains honor* by kneeling down and washing feet. The Pharisees seek to be served rather than to serve, loving the places of honor at banquets and basking in the attention drawn by their priestly garb. The Pharisees speak *about God*, whereas Jesus *is God*—yet they consider Him their rival.

The religious leaders are *envious* of Jesus' popularity. They are also *jealous* that Jesus is attracting their followers who are now following Him. The miracles, the crowds, the Truth are more than they can tolerate. Ultimately, their envy prompts them to plot a devious plan—the death of Jesus. If they cannot have what they want, they will kill the One who has what they want—even if it means killing the Christ, the Messiah, "the Anointed One." With grave concern they acknowledge, *"Here is this man performing many signs."*

> **"So from that day on**
> **they plotted to take his life."**
> **(John 11:47, 53)**

Key Verses to Memorize

Fast forward to the period of time following the death of Jesus and the birth of the church. In Philippians 3:5–6, we see one famous Pharisee with all the "right" credentials: *"circumcised on the eighth day, of the people of Israel, of the tribe of Benjamin, a Hebrew of Hebrews."* And the list goes on. *"As for zeal, persecuting the church; as for righteousness . . . faultless."*

However, his zeal is misplaced in man-made traditions and religious ritual rather than in a Person—the living God. Then one day, he comes face-to-face with the risen Christ, and his life completely changes. Now Paul realizes, *"Whatever gain I had, I counted as loss for the sake of Christ"* (Philippians 3:7 ESV).

Eventually Paul discovers a secret—the spiritual *secret* called "contentment." He describes finding *contentment* in Christ and ridding himself of his pharisaical trappings.

> *"I know what it is to be in need,*
> *and I know what it is to have plenty.*
> *I have learned the secret of being content in*
> *any and every situation, whether well fed or*
> *hungry, whether living in plenty or in want.*
> *I can do all this through him*
> *who gives me strength."*
> (Philippians 4:12–13)

Key Passage to Read

As a master storyteller, Jesus often uses *parables* to communicate "an earthly story with a heavenly meaning."

In His "Parable of the Vineyard Workers," different day laborers are offered work for pay at five different times of the day (the 1st, 3rd, 6th, 9th, and 11th hours). Those who work the full day will be paid appropriately for their work. They feel content—completely content with the agreed upon compensation—until they learn that those who worked only a partial day receive the same wage as those working the full day. Immediately, *their contentment turned to resentment!*

"It's not fair!" they grumbled. "How dare the landowner pay identical wages—especially to those who did not work identical hours!"

The following parable is filled with the common problems of misplaced expectations, complaining, and resentment in contrast to the generous gift of grace.

MATTHEW 20:1–16

▶ **Envy** is caused by misplaced *expectations* (vv. 8–10).

"When evening came, the owner of the vineyard said to his foreman, 'Call the workers and pay them their wages, beginning with the last ones hired and going on to the first.' The workers

hired about five in the afternoon came and each received a denarius. So when those came who were hired first, they expected to receive more. But each one of them also received a denarius" (Matthew 20:8–10).

▶ **Envy** causes ***grumbling*** (vv. 11–12).

"They began to grumble against the landowner. 'These who were hired last worked only one hour,' they said, 'and you have made them equal to us who have borne the burden of the work and the heat of the day'" (Matthew 20:11–12).

▶ **Envy** focuses on what appears ***unfair*** (vv. 13–14).

"He answered one of them, 'I am not being unfair to you, friend. Didn't you agree to work for a denarius? Take your pay and go'" (Matthew 20:13–14).

▶ **Envy** resents ***generosity*** that others receive (vv. 14–16).

"I want to give the one who was hired last the same as I gave you. Don't I have the right to do what I want with my own money? Or are you envious because I am generous? So the last will be first, and the first will be last" (Matthew 20:14–16).

In real life, not everyone will be treated "fairly." At times, some people will be treated with unusual generosity. (That's the nature of God who gives us *grace*—meaning a gift we don't deserve.)

The Point of This Parable

The *earthly meaning*: Beware of envy—it will turn your contentment into resentment.

The *heavenly meaning*: We don't "earn" God's favor. Rather, we simply receive His unearned favor bestowed on us because He delights in giving His children "good gifts." If we desire true contentment, our focus must not be in looking horizontally, comparing ourselves with others, but looking vertically at our relationship with our Redeemer—the God of all grace (1 Peter 5:10). One day, when every authentic Christian is living in the physical kingdom of heaven, we will be in absolute awe at His matchless mercy (not getting what we do deserve) and filled with utter gratitude for His gift of grace upon grace upon grace—above and beyond what we could ever imagine.

One way of understanding this passage is . . .

Any laborer [anyone] *who accepts the invitation* [to become a Christian] *from the Landowner* [God Himself] *to come into the vineyard* [into His heavenly kingdom], *no matter how late in the day* [late in life], *will be as equally and generously rewarded* [with eternal life] *as those who have labored* [been consistently faithful] *the longest.*

The emotions of envy and jealousy essentially boil down to a case of the *haves* and the *have nots* who also want to be the *haves.*

Picture a tug-of-war rope: At one end, jealousy guards what it has and stubbornly holds on for dear life. At the other end, envy yearns for what it doesn't have and grasps to gain ground. Neither one wins the prize, for the struggle wears on those already weary and tears apart what once was whole.

Resentful envy and bitter jealousy are much like our enemy on the prowl, seeking to destroy like *"roaring lions that tear their prey open"* (Psalm 22:13). We are warned to *"Be alert and of sober mind. Your enemy the devil prowls around like a roaring lion looking for someone to devour"* (1 Peter 5:8).

But God doesn't want us to fall prey to the traps of envy and jealousy. Instead, He offers His formula for freedom—the target of transformation. And His Word assures that such change is possible, for . . .

> **"Jesus replied,**
> **'What is impossible with man**
> **is possible with God.'"**
> **(Luke 18:27)**

Reaching the Target: Transformation!

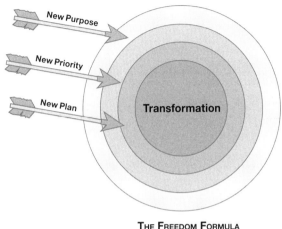

The Freedom Formula

A New Purpose
+ A New Priority
+ A New Plan
———————————
A Transformed Life

Target 1—A New Purpose: God's purpose for me is to be conformed to the character of Christ.

"Those God foreknew he also predestined to be conformed to the image of his Son" (Romans 8:29).

- "I'll do whatever it takes to be conformed to the character of Christ."

Target 2—A New Priority: God's priority for me is to change my thinking.

"Do not conform to the pattern of this world, but be transformed by the renewing of your mind" (Romans 12:2).

- "I'll do whatever it takes to line up my thinking with God's thinking.

Target 3—A New Plan: God's plan for me is to rely on Christ's strength, not my strength, to be all He created me to be.

> *"I can do all things through Christ who strengthens me"* (Philippians 4:13 NKJV).

- "I'll do whatever it takes to fulfill His plan in His strength."

My Personalized Plan[12]

When I doubt God's perfect plan and provision for me, I leave myself open to wrong assumptions and conclusions. To overcome envy and jealousy, I must root out the seeds of doubt and discontentment that threaten the peace God promises. To do that, I will fight . . .

▶ ARROGANCE

"Because God is the Source of what I have, I don't deserve more than I have, nor even deserve what I do have. I humbly acknowledge that the abilities I have are actually a gift from God."

> *"What do you have that God hasn't given you? And if everything you have is from God, why boast as though it were not a gift?"* (1 Corinthians 4:7 NLT)

► COMPARISON

"Because God made me as I am, I will stop comparing my strengths and weaknesses to others. I will remember that God reveals His strength through my weakness."

"He said to me, 'My grace is sufficient for you, for my power is made perfect in weakness.' Therefore I will boast all the more gladly about my weaknesses, so that Christ's power may rest on me" (2 Corinthians 12:9).

► COMPETITION

"Because God created everyone in His image, I don't have to compete with others to prove myself. I will choose to care about others rather than compete with others."

"In humility value others above yourselves, not looking to your own interests but each of you to the interests of the others" (Philippians 2:3–4).

► COVETOUSNESS

"Because God commands me not to covet, I refuse to obsess over what others have. Instead, I'll be thankful for what I have in this life."

"Since we are receiving a kingdom that cannot be shaken, let us be thankful" (Hebrews 12:28).

► DENIAL

"Because God desires that I walk in truth, I will confess my sin when I allow envy or jealousy to reside in my heart. I will change my thoughts and ask God to purify my heart from all that is not right in His sight."

"If we claim to be without sin, we deceive ourselves and the truth is not in us. If we confess our sins, he is faithful and just and will forgive us our sins and purify us from all unrighteousness" (1 John 1:8–9).

▶ DISCONTENT

"Because God doesn't want to withhold what is good for me, I will be content with everything God has provided me."

"For the LORD God is a sun and shield; the LORD bestows favor and honor; no good thing does he withhold from those whose walk is blameless" (Psalm 84:11).

▶ DISSATISFACTION

"Because God knows what is best for me, I will trust in Him and be satisfied that He will meet my needs. I will resist the urge to 'want it *all*.'"

"The LORD will guide you always; he will satisfy your needs in a sun-scorched land and will strengthen your frame. You will be like a well-watered garden, like a spring whose waters never fail" (Isaiah 58:11).

▶ FEAR

"Because I'm promised God's strong help for my life, I will not fear the changes He allows. I will trust Him to help me and calm my fear."

"Do not fear, for I am with you; do not be dismayed, for I am your God. I will strengthen you and help you; I will uphold you with my righteous right hand" (Isaiah 41:10).

▶ INSECURITY

"Because I have God's unfailing love and guidance, I will not rely on a false sense of security that comes from people or things. I will not put my trust in what I have, but will entrust my life to the Lord."

"Let the morning bring me word of your unfailing love, for I have put my trust in you. Show me the way I should go, for to you I entrust my life" (Psalm 143:8).

▶ PRIDE

"Because God is God and I am not, I will examine my motives to determine what problem I am trying to resolve through envy and jealousy. I will acknowledge that I cannot control everything in my life, but I can trust and bow down to the only One who can. He saves me—even from myself."

"You shall have no other gods before me . . . for I, the LORD your God, am a jealous God" (Exodus 20:3, 5).

Any one of us can carry resentment in our hearts which is created by destructive envy. This negative emotion is not only poisonous to us, but it can also infect our most meaningful relationships, including our relationship with God. This should be motivation enough for us to find a way to replace our resentment with grace and gratitude.

> **"Let the message about Christ,**
> **in all its richness, fill your lives.**
> **Teach and counsel each other**
> **with all the wisdom he gives.**
> **Sing psalms and hymns and spiritual**
> **songs to God with thankful hearts."**
> **(Colossians 3:16 NLT)**

▶ **Face your feelings** of resentment and use them as indicators of your need to change.

"Lord, I admit my selfish, resentful feelings and admit I need to be rid of them."

"If you harbor bitter envy and selfish ambition in your hearts, do not boast about it or deny the truth" (James 3:14).

▶ **Recognize the source** of the self-centered emotion of envy.

"Lord, help me to look below the surface to see my self-centered desires and fears. Turn my focus from me to You."

"Turn my heart toward your statutes and not toward selfish gain" (Psalm 119:36).

▶ **Eliminate the emotion** of envy.

"Lord, instead of being controlled by envy, help me be controlled only by Your love."

"The love of Christ controls us, because we have concluded this: that one has died for all, therefore all have died" (2 Corinthians 5:14 ESV).

▶ **Be sure your thinking** lines up with God's thinking—now and in the future.

"Lord, thank You for allowing me to be a steward of everything You've placed in my care. I admit my dissatisfaction is not caused by another person but by my decision to hold on to false feelings of failure and diminished self-worth. Everything I have belongs to you, including me."

"'The silver is mine and the gold is mine,' declares the Lord Almighty" (Haggai 2:8).

▶ **Turn your focus** from *receiving from* others to *giving to* others.

"Lord, I will look for ways to express Your love to others in unexpected ways, at unexpected times, without expecting anything in return."

"It is more blessed to give than to receive" (Acts 20:35).

A crowd gathers outside the governor's palace. Pilate observes as the envious religious leaders incite disorder and anger. Should he release the criminal Barabbas? The overwhelming cry is *yes!* The mob chooses to set free the murderer rather than the Messiah. And the collective call for Jesus? *"Crucify him!"* And Pilate complies in order to pacify.

> **"Wanting to satisfy the crowd, Pilate released Barabbas to them. He had Jesus flogged, and handed him over to be crucified." (Mark 15:15)**

▶ **Be sure to replace your jealousy** with God's unconditional *agape love.*[13]

"The entire law is fulfilled in keeping this one command: 'Love [agape] your neighbor as yourself'" (Galatians 5:14).

- *Agape love* enables us to seek the highest good of another.

"I will earnestly pray, 'Lord, I will do what is in the best interest of (Name).' "

"My command is this: Love each other as I have loved you" (John 15:12).

- *Agape love* keeps us from expecting too much from another.

"I commit myself to be patient and kind, not envious or self-seeking."

"Love is patient, love is kind. It does not envy, it does not boast, it is not proud. It does not dishonor others, it is not self-seeking, it is not easily angered, it keeps no record of wrongs" (1 Corinthians 13:4–5).

- *Agape love* guards us from expecting everything to always go our way in this life.

  "I realize that this life is temporary—I will not expect to have total fulfillment until I live with the Lord in eternity."

  "We fix our eyes not on what is seen, but on what is unseen, since what is seen is temporary, but what is unseen is eternal" (2 Corinthians 4:18).

▶ **Be sure your *plans* line up with God's plan.**

- Remember that God has a good purpose for all He does and a reason for all He plans.

- Be content with God's plan for your life.

- Stop making comparisons that cause anxiety, depression, and loss of self-esteem.

"Rich and poor have this in common: The Lord is the Maker of them all" (Proverbs 22:2).

▶ **Be sure your *priorities* line up with God's priorities as found in His Word.**

- Don't focus on *your* plan, but on *God's* plan for you.

- Submit your will to His will.

- Make it your goal to please Him with all you have and all you do.

"We make it our goal to please him, whether we are at home in the body or away from it" (2 Corinthians 5:9).

▶ **Be sure your *peace*** lines up with the God's peace.

- Thank God for all He has allowed you to have.

- Hold everything and everyone with an open hand before God.

- Realize no one has everything.

"Do not be anxious about anything, but in every situation, by prayer and petition, with thanksgiving, present your requests to God. And the peace of God, which transcends all understanding, will guard your hearts and your minds in Christ Jesus" (Philippians 4:6–7).

▶ **Be sure your *perspective*** lines up with God's perspective.

- Fix your eyes on an eternal perspective to help keep temporary things from ruling your life.

- Renew your perspective with God's by daily reading and reflecting on His Word.

- Pray, "Lord, I'll do whatever it takes to be conformed to the character of Christ."

"Let us strip off every weight that slows us down, especially the sin that so easily trips us up. And let us run with endurance the race God has set before us. We do this by keeping our eyes on Jesus, the champion who initiates and perfects our faith" (Hebrews 12:1–2 NLT).

How the religious leaders respond to the miracle before their very eyes is simply inconceivable. Jesus encounters a man with a shriveled hand. The all-knowing Son of God realizes that the Pharisees are looking for a way to trap Him. They watch and wonder if He will heal on this day—on the Sabbath.

Jesus tells the man to stand in front of everyone and then asks the envious and jealous Pharisees a pointed, purposeful question. *"Which is lawful on the Sabbath: to do good or to do evil, to save life or to kill?"* (Mark 3:4). But like an arrow ricocheting off stone, the question fails to penetrate their hardened hearts, and they seethe in silence. Angry and deeply distressed, Jesus' eyes rove from one Pharisee's face to the next. The Son of God's attention then returns to the need at hand—*to do good* and not evil. He tells the man to stretch out his hand, and his hand is completely restored.

A miraculous healing occurs—a synagogue worshipper will no longer experience the encumbrance of a deformed hand—but how do the religious leaders react? Is there an attitude of gratitude for Jesus' gracious act? Does praise spill forth from the Pharisees' lips?

No, their response is riddled with envy: *"Then the Pharisees went out and began to plot with the Herodians how they might kill Jesus"* (Mark 3:6).

Gaining an Attitude of Gratitude

God, who knows all things, knows envy and jealousy are rooted in selfishness and pride and in the idea that He is unfair, unjust, and unsympathetic in His actions toward us. Some believe that He is *partial* to certain people and *impartial* to others or that He *should* distribute material wealth, physical and emotional health, professional and relational success, talents and abilities equally to all of His people.

Yet who are we to judge the rightness of God's plans? He is not creating inequality by varying the gifts He gives. Rather, He is building a body made up of many parts, each having equal value. God tells us to look at the bigger picture and embrace it, for therein lies contentment and the motivation to relish the role He's called us to live out.

> "Just as a body, though one,
> has many parts . . . so it is with Christ.
> God has placed the parts in the body . . .
> just as he wanted them to be . . . so that
> there should be no division in the body,
> but that its parts should have equal
> concern for each other."
> (1 Corinthians 12:12, 18, 25)

▶ **Look at what God has placed in your own hands** rather than what is in the hands of others.

- Begin and end each day expressing thanks to God for at least one thing.

- Maintain an attitude of gratitude to God throughout the day.

"They were also to stand every morning to thank and praise the LORD. They were to do the same in the evening" (1 Chronicles 23:30).

▶ **Look at what God has done *for* you in the past** rather than what He has done for others.

- Create a timeline of your life in ten-year increments.

- As you think back over the events in your past, note on your timeline the times you know you were blessed by God and thank Him for each one.

"I remember the days of long ago; I meditate on all your works and consider what your hands have done" (Psalm 143:5).

▶ **Look at what God is doing *in* you** rather than what He is doing in others.

- Prayerfully ask God to show you ways He is working in your life to mold and shape your character to reflect the character of Christ.

- Thank Him for preparing you for greater service, and ask Him to make you a godly example to those whose lives you touch.

"It is God who works in you to will and to act in order to fulfill his good purpose" (Philippians 2:13).

▶ **Look at what God is doing *through* you** rather than what He is doing through others.

- Enlist the help of someone who knows you well to help evaluate your gifts, talents, and abilities.

- Examine how you are expressing the love of God to loved ones, strangers, and those in the body of Christ, His church.

"We always thank God for all of you and continually mention you in our prayers. We remember before our God and Father your work produced by faith, your labor prompted by love, and your endurance inspired by hope in our Lord Jesus Christ. . . . you became a model to all the believers . . . your faith in God has become known everywhere" (1 Thessalonians 1:2–3, 7–8).

Look at what God has promised *regarding* you rather than what He has promised regarding others.

- Become familiar with the promises of God to those who place their faith in Jesus Christ.

- Write out the promises that touch your heart and personalize each one.

"His divine power has given us everything we need for a godly life through our knowledge of him who called us by his own glory and goodness. Through these he has given us his very great and precious promises, so that through them you may participate in the divine nature, having escaped the corruption in the world caused by evil desires" (2 Peter 1:3–4).

Even after Jesus' death, resurrection, and ascension
back to heaven, the religious leaders remain jealous.
The apostle Paul, a Pharisee until he encounters
the resurrected Christ, continually reasons from
the Scriptures, *"explaining and proving that the
Messiah had to suffer and rise from the dead. 'This
Jesus I am proclaiming to you is the Messiah,' he said"*
(Acts 17:3).

The gospel message does not fall on deaf ears as
some Jews and *"a large number of God-fearing
Greeks and quite a few prominent women"*
(Acts 17:4) become believers. The Bible says, *"But
other Jews were jealous; so they rounded up some
bad characters from the marketplace, formed a mob
and started a riot in the city"* (Acts 17:5). They incite
further jealousy among the Romans by accusing
Paul and his fellow servants of defying Caesar's
decrees for claiming another king, *one named Jesus.*

Nevertheless, in spite of their jealousy, Paul knows
the importance of *confrontation that is tactful,
tempered*, and *timely* when he gives these words
of wisdom.

> "Let your conversation be always
> full of grace, seasoned with salt,
> so that you may know
> how to answer everyone."
> (Colossians 4:6)

Steps to Confrontation

If you are led by the Lord to confront a jealous person—even one jealous of you—put these ground rules in place.

▶ **Confront in love**—speak in love.

- "I care about you. I sense that you fear a real loss in your life. Am I right?"

"The wise in heart are called discerning, and gracious words promote instruction" (Proverbs 16:21).

▶ **Determine the cause** of the jealousy—is it selfish jealousy or godly jealousy?

- If the jealousy is caused by a genuine threat to a covenant relationship—like within a marriage—then it is godly.

- If the jealousy is caused by a possessive desire to control another person—especially when that person should be free to make independent choices—then it is selfish.

Love is not selfish or controlling but seeks what is best for the person loved. God loves you enough to give you freedom to choose or reject Him. The true test of your love for others is if you will grant them freedom.

"Love is patient and kind. Love is not jealous or boastful or proud" (1 Corinthians 13:4 NLT).

▶ **Decide whether the jealousy is justified**, a product of a fearful imagination, or an underlying sense of insecurity. (Is there a true threat of loss?)

- "On what facts are your feelings based?"

"All a person's ways seem pure to them, but motives are weighed by the LORD" (Proverbs 16:2).

▶ **Encourage disclosure** of the emotional pain being experienced without placing blame.

- Ask gently probing questions.

"What painful thoughts and feelings are you having?"

"The purposes of a person's heart are deep waters, but one who has insight draws them out" (Proverbs 20:5).

▶ **Ask forgiveness** for any possible offenses—do not be defensive.

- If the person is jealous of you for justified reasons, admit your wrongs and ask forgiveness.

"I realize I have wronged you by my lack of sensitivity. Would you please forgive me?"

"Bear with each other and forgive one another if any of you has a grievance against someone. Forgive as the Lord forgave you" (Colossians 3:13).

▶ **Affirm the jealous person** by giving genuine praise and encouragement.

- Verbalize the person's positive qualities and affirm your commitment to the relationship.

"I appreciate your willingness to be open and honest with me, and am confident God will help you through this and help me to make the changes I need to make."

"Encourage one another and build each other up, just as in fact you are doing" (1 Thessalonians 5:11).

▶ **Work on a plan** together.

- Help decide what to pray and what to say when jealous feelings erupt.

"Let's ask God to direct each of us to Scriptures that will help us deal with jealousy—so we know what to say to each other and how to pray if these feelings come up again."

"Plans fail for lack of counsel, but with many advisers they succeed" (Proverbs 15:22).

▶ **Withdraw** from one who is demonstrating open hatred or angry, destructive manipulation.

- Communicate your intent to withdraw and a willingness to try again later.

"It is not healthy for me to listen to anger that is out of control. We'll talk later when you're not angry."

"Do not make friends with a hot-tempered person, do not associate with one easily angered" (Proverbs 22:24).

HOW TO Set Boundaries with Someone Excessively Jealous

Excessive jealousy leads to excessive control. This inappropriate jealousy—though couched as "protective and caring"—is actually demoralizing and damaging. Jealous people wield much power.

Excessive jealousy is typically rooted in excessive fear and tightly tied to former experiences of rejection from childhood. Until those former experiences are resolved and released, success will be illusive. There will continue to be situations that trigger fear associated with past experiences resulting in over-controlling jealousy.

Time and space followed by a direct "take charge" approach is required to diffuse it and free the one ensnared by it. If you give it an inch, it will take a mile.

> "My eyes are ever on the Lord,
> for only he will release my feet
> from the snare."
> (Psalm 25:15)

Statements for Setting Boundaries

In setting a boundary with someone who is excessively jealous, consider using the following conversational approach to help establish a healthy relationship.

▶**Validate** the relationship.

"I care deeply about you, and our relationship is important to me."

▶**Ask** for agreement in repairing the relationship.

"Are you willing to work toward what God would want for us in an emotionally healthy relationship?"

▶**Identify** what needs to change.

"I am concerned about your jealousy. Your anger and possessiveness must stop if you want our relationship to survive."

▶**State** what is acceptable and what is not.

"Because our relationship is important to both of us, we need to talk about issues calmly and rationally instead of in anger and with harshness."

▶**Define** what acceptable communication means to you.

"Talking calmly and rationally means we will not yell at each other or accuse one another. We will discuss what we think and feel and ask the Lord to help us communicate effectively."

▶ **Explain** appropriate behavior.

"I want to spend time with you, but you must understand that I also need time to be by myself and explore interests of my own, and time with healthy people who are important to me."

▶ **Establish** boundaries about how you expect to be treated.

"I will no longer subject myself to unjustified, irrational accusations. If you choose to act in a jealous manner as you have in the past, I will leave for a time to allow you to cool off."

▶ **State** consequences for violating boundaries.

"If you will not do this, understand that I will continue to withdraw from you until you are willing to work through our issues rather than act jealously. If you cannot honor my boundaries, I will continue to withdraw from you. I pray that you get help through wise counsel, either together with me or on your own."

▶ **Maintain** boundaries even when they have been broken.

"You have chosen to _____, and I explained before that the repercussion is _____."

▶ **Reinforce** repercussions.

"Because you have chosen to ignore my boundaries, you are choosing the repercussions as well. I am only doing what I said I would do. Please let me know if you are willing to change your behavior in order for us to have the best relationship possible."

▶ **Continue** maintaining boundaries and impose stronger repercussions.

"I care about you, but the only way we can continue our relationship will be if these issues are resolved. If we are not able to do that on our own, I will insist on outside help, such as a counselor. If you are unwilling to do that to save our relationship, then you will be choosing to end it."

"Above all else, guard your heart, for everything you do flows from it." (Proverbs 4:23)

When you focus on the blessings of others instead of your own, envy and jealousy obscure your view of the gifts God has given you.

You question God's goodness and lose your sense of love, joy, and peace.

But when you choose to practice contentment, you demonstrate your trust in the Lord.

—JUNE HUNT

Comparison or Contentment?

When we find ourselves prone to envy or jealousy and compare ourselves or even our possessions, we often see our own glass as half-empty rather than half-full. But what if the tables were turned and we chose to see how our status could stir jealousy in others or our situation could be one others might envy? What if you choose to quit comparing and instead choose to embrace true contentment?

Imagine living your life without being able to walk, care for your own needs, or even embrace those you love. How would you view yourself if you were born without arms and legs? Would you be able to cope with the challenges your physical condition presented? Consider not only dealing with the typical traumas of school and adolescence, but also struggling with depression and loneliness because your differences are so very different.

Born in 1982 in Australia, Nick Vujicic's parents had no warning, no medical explanation, and no idea how to care for their infant son born missing his arms and legs. His disability was so severe that at age 10, he attempted to take his own life by drowning. But he couldn't carry through with his plan because he couldn't bear the thought of the pain this would cause his parents and brother who loved him. At age 15, the Lord revealed Himself to Nick, and he found purpose and meaning for his life.

Since age 19, Nick has traveled the world, sharing his story with millions of souls desperate for God's grace. He's an accomplished author, musician, devoted husband, and dedicated father. Incredibly, his hobbies include fishing, painting, and swimming. Today this vibrant young evangelist has accomplished much more than anyone might have ever expected from someone with his physical limitations. Yet Nick has achieved a great deal more than many do in a lifetime without any physical limitations at all.

Nick credits his strength and passion for life today to his faith in God through his relationship with Jesus Christ. Nick says, "If God can use a man without arms and legs to be His hands and feet, then He will certainly use any willing heart!"[14]

When your heart is willing, God is able to help you eliminate envy and jealousy. When you stop trying to see how you stack up to others, when you quit comparing who you are, what you have, and what you want, you will be able to look at your own life and remember *Whose* you are.

> "Godliness with contentment
> is great gain.
> For we brought nothing into the world,
> and we can take nothing out of it."
> (1 Timothy 6:6–7)

SCRIPTURES TO MEMORIZE

If **love is patient** and **kind**, what **does not** exhibit love?

*"**Love is patient, love is kind**. It **does not envy**, it does not boast, it is not proud"* (1 Corinthians 13:4).

What emotion should I avoid when I see **those who are evil** or **those who do wrong**?

*"Do not fret because of **those who are evil** or be **envious** of **those who do wrong**"* (Psalm 37:1).

What emotions are **cruel** and **overwhelming**? What is even harder to **stand** against?

*"Anger is **cruel** and fury **overwhelming**, but who can **stand** before jealousy?"* (Proverbs 27:4).

What do **you find** where there is **envy and selfish ambition**?

*"For where you have **envy and selfish ambition**, there **you find** disorder and every evil practice"* (James 3:16).

What **rots** the **bones**?

*"A heart at peace gives life to the body, but **envy rots the bones**"* (Proverbs 14:30).

Of what should you be sure to **rid yourself**?

*"**Rid yourselves** of all malice and all deceit, hypocrisy, **envy**, and slander of every kind"* (1 Peter 2:1).

When **there is jealousy**, what is the result?

*"For since **there is jealousy** and quarreling among you, are you not worldly?"* (1 Corinthians 3:3).

Is there **anything that belongs to your neighbor** that is permissible to **covet**?

*"You shall **not covet** . . . **anything that belongs to your neighbor**"* (Exodus 20:17).

To what extent should **I have learned to be content**?

*"**I have learned to be content** whatever the circumstances"* (Philippians 4:11).

Is there anything to **gain** if I choose **godliness** and **contentment** in my life?

*"**Godliness** with **contentment** is great **gain**"* (1 Timothy 6:6).

NOTES

1. *Merriam-Webster Collegiate Dictionary* (2001); http://www.m-w.com.

2. W. E. Vine, Merrill Unger, William White, *Vine's Complete Expository Dictionary of Biblical Words* (Nashville: Thomas Nelson, 1996), 204.

3. Vine, Unger, White, *Vine's Complete Expository Dictionary of Biblical Words*, 136.

4. Merriam Webster, "jealous."

5. W. E. Vine, Merrill Unger, William White, *Vine's Complete Expository Dictionary of Biblical Words* electronic ed. (Nashville: Thomas Nelson, 1996)

6. Vine, Unger, White, *Vine's Complete Expository Dictionary of Biblical Words*, 136.

7. Betsy Cohen, *The Snow White Syndrome: All About Envy* (New York: Macmillan, 1986), 23–24; Charles R. Swindoll, *Killing Giants, Pulling Thorns* (Portland, Ore.: Multnomah, 1978), 23.

8. Cohen, *The Snow White Syndrome*, 25.

9. This section adapted from Doug Britton, "Evaluate Yourself if Your Spouse Is Jealous," *Life Tree* (Citrus Heights, CA), accessed May 8, 2015, http://www.dougbrittonbooks.com/onlinebiblestudies-depressionanddiscouragement/jealousyandinsecurity-evaluateyourselfifyourspouseisjealous.php.

10. Lawrence J. Crabb, Jr., *Understanding People: Deep Longings for Relationship*, Ministry Resources Library (Grand Rapids: Zondervan, 1987), 15–16; Robert S. McGee, *The Search for Significance*, 2nd ed. (Houston, TX: Rapha, 1990), 27–30.

11. Crabb, Jr., *Understanding People*, 15-16; McGee, *The Search for Significance*, 27-30.

12. Alice Fryling, *Reshaping a Jealous Heart* (Downers Grove, IL: InterVarsity Press, 1994), 15-17.

13. Horst Robert Balz and Gerhard Schneider, *Exegetical Dictionary of the New Testament*, Translation of: *Exegetisches Worterbuch zum Neuen Testament*, volume 1 (Grand Rapids, Mich.: Eerdmans, 1993), 8–12.

14. This section adapted from "Nick," *LifeWithoutLimbs* (Agoura Hills, CA), accessed August 1, 2017, https://www.lifewithoutlimbs.org/about-nick/bio/.

HOPE FOR THE HEART TITLES

- *Adultery*
- *Aging Well*
- *Alcohol & Drug Abuse*
- *Anger*
- *Anorexia & Bulimia*
- *Boundaries*
- *Bullying*
- *Caregiving*
- *Chronic Illness & Disability*
- *Codependency*
- *Conflict Resolution*
- *Confrontation*
- *Considering Marriage*
- *Critical Spirit*
- *Decision Making*
- *Depression*
- *Domestic Violence*
- *Dysfunctional Family*
- *Envy & Jealousy*
- *Fear*
- *Financial Freedom*
- *Forgiveness*
- *Friendship*
- *Gambling*
- *Grief*
- *Guilt*
- *Hope*
- *Loneliness*
- *Manipulation*
- *Marriage*
- *Overeating*
- *Parenting*
- *Perfectionism*
- *Procrastination*
- *Reconciliation*
- *Rejection*
- *Self-Worth*
- *Sexual Integrity*
- *Singleness*
- *Spiritual Abuse*
- *Stress*
- *Success Through Failure*
- *Suicide Prevention*
- *Trials*
- *Verbal & Emotional Abuse*
- *Victimization*